FESTIVE FOODS
CHINA

Sylvia Goulding

CHELSEA
CLUBHOUSE
An Imprint of Chelsea House Publishers

Chelsea Clubhouse
An imprint of Chelsea House Publishers
132 West 31st Street
New York, NY 10001

Library of Congress Cataloging-in-Publication Data

Goulding, Sylvia.
  Festive foods / Sylvia Goulding. – 1st ed.
    v. cm.
  Includes bibliographical references and index.
  Contents: [1] China – [2] France – [3] Germany – [4] India – [5] Italy – [6] Japan – [7] Mexico – [8] United States.
  ISBN 978-0-7910-9751-9 (v. 1) – ISBN 978-0-7910-9752-6 (v. 2) – ISBN 978-0-7910-9756-4 (v. 3) – ISBN 978-0-7910-9757-1 (v. 4) – ISBN 978-0-7910-9753-3 (v. 5) – ISBN 978-0-7910-9754-0 (v. 6) – ISBN 978-0-7910-9755-7 (v. 7) – ISBN 978-0-7910-9758-8 (v. 8)
  1. Cookery, International. 2. Gardening. 3. Manners and customs. I. Title.
  TX725.A1G56 2008
  641.59–dc22

                              2007042722

Chelsea Clubhouse books are available at special discounts when purchased in bulk quantities for businesses, associations, institutions, or sales promotions. Please call our Special Sales Department in New York at (212) 967-8800 or (800) 322-8755.

You can find Chelsea Clubhouse on the World Wide Web at **http://www.chelseahouse.com**

Printed and bound in Dubai

10 9 8 7 6 5 4 3 2 1

For The Brown Reference Group plc.:
Project Editor: Sylvia Goulding
Cooking Editor: Angelika Ilies
Contributors: Jacqueline Fortey, Sylvia Goulding
Photographers: Klaus Arras, Lucy Suleiman
Cartographer: Darren Awuah
Art Editor: Paula Keogh
Illustrator: Jo Gracie
Picture Researcher: Mike Goulding
Managing Editor: Bridget Giles
Production Director: Alastair Gourlay
Editorial Director: Lindsey Lowe
Children's Publisher: Anne O'Daly

Photographic Credits:
Front Cover: Shutterstock (inset); Klaus Arras (main)
Back Cover: Klaus Arras
Alamy Barry Lewis 6, Keren Su/China Span 9, LMR Group 14; **iStock** 4; **Paula Keogh** 7; **Shutterstock** title page, 3, 5, 7, 8, 10, 11, 12, 13, 15, 20, 21, 22, 23, 24, 25, 28, 29, 30, 31, 32, 35, 36, 37, 38, 39, 40, 43

With thanks to models:
Caspar, Hannah, Jeremy, Mariam, and Miho

Cooking Editor
Angelika Ilies has always been interested in cookery and other countries. She studied nutritional sciences in college. She has lived in the United States, England, and Germany. She has also traveled extensively and collected international recipes on her journeys. Angelika has written more than 70 cookbooks and cooking card series. She currently lives in Frankfurt, Germany, with her two children and has spent much time researching children's nutrition. Both children regularly cook with their mother.

Contents

let's START COOKING

Cooking is fun—you learn about different ingredients and cooking methods, you find out how things taste, and you can serve a meal to your family and friends that you have cooked yourself! Some of the recipes in this book have steps that need adult help—ask a parent or other adult if they will be your kitchen assistant while you cook a meal.

This line tells you how many people the meal will feed.

In this box, you find out which ingredients you need for your meal.

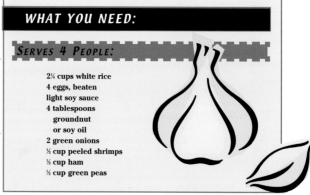

WHAT YOU NEED:

SERVES 4 PEOPLE:

2¼ cups white rice
4 eggs, beaten
light soy sauce
4 tablespoons
   groundnut
   or soy oil
2 green onions
⅓ cup peeled shrimps
⅓ cup ham
⅓ cup green peas

Check before you start that you have everything at home. If something is missing, write it on your shopping list. Get all the ingredients ready before you start cooking.

◁ We all share tasks in the kitchen, from chopping the vegetables and cooking them to arranging the food in a dish to serve.

! WHEN TO GET help

Most cooking involves cutting ingredients and heating them in some way, whether frying, boiling, or cooking in the oven. Each time you see this exclamation mark, be extra careful as you cook and make sure your adult kitchen assistant is around to help.

For many meals you need to chop an onion. First cut off a thin slice at both ends. Pull off the peel. Cut the onion in half from end to end. Put one half with the cut side down on the chopping board. Hold it with one hand and cut end-to-end slices with the other hand. Hold the slices together and cut across the slices to make small cubes. Make sure you do not cut yourself!

Other recipes in this book use fresh chilies. Always wear rubber or surgical gloves when chopping chilies. If you don't have any gloves, wash your hands very thoroughly afterward, and do not touch your skin for a while. Chili seeds and the white pith contain a substance that makes your skin burn. Trim off the stalk and halve the chili lengthways. Scrape out the seeds and throw them away.

A **wok** is a Chinese cooking pan. It has a round bottom, high sides, and a handle. Woks are used for stir-frying.

This is a Chinese **soup spoon**. People use it to eat a soup or a liquid dish. You can use an ordinary spoon instead.

Bamboo steamers are used for cooking different foods at the same time. Each ring holds one dish. They are stacked and set over a pan of boiling hot water.

Chopsticks are what Chinese people use instead of knives and forks to eat their food. It is fun to try using them, but you can use a knife, fork, or spoon instead.

A trip around
CHINA

China's food is loved around the world. Unlike the United States, China has many neighbors: Mongolia to the north, Russia, Kazakhstan, Pakistan, and Afghanistan to the west, Nepal, Bhutan, Myanmar, India, Laos, Cambodia, and Vietnam to the south, and North Korea to the east. Hong Kong forms part of a group of islands off China's southeastern coast. China's capital, Beijing, is on the northern edge of the North China Plain. China has twenty-three provinces, five autonomous regions, and four municipalities. The Great Wall of China snakes along mountains to the west of Beijing.

A variety of climates

China's climate varies from very cold in the north to hot and humid in the south. Heavy rainfalls called monsoons and dangerous storms called typhoons are common in the south.

△ **More than 1.3 billion people** live in China—that is 4½ times as many people as live in the United States. China's main language is a form of Chinese called Standard Mandarin.

NORTH AMERICA

EUROPE

ASIA

AFRICA

CHINA

SOUTHEAST ASIA

◁ **China** is the world's third-largest country, after Russia and Canada. It is located in the east of the Asian continent. Its long coast borders the Pacific Ocean.

1

中华人民共和国万岁   世界人民大团结万岁

△ **Beijing** is the capital of the People's Republic of China. After Shanghai, it is the country's second largest city. In the center of Beijing is the Forbidden City, the former emperor's palace.

RUSSIAN FEDERATION

KAZAKHSTAN

MONGOLIA

XINJIANG

INNER MONGOLIA

KYRGYZSTAN

Korla ●

Huang He (Yellow River)

BEIJING ●

N. KOREA

TAJIKISTAN

● Yinchuan

1

Yellow Sea

PAKISTAN

CHINA

● Xining

S. KOREA

INDIA

XIZANG

JAPAN

Three Gorges Dam

SICHUAN

● Wuhan

● Shanghai

Chang Jiang (Yangtze)

East China Sea

2

2

NEPAL

BHUTAN

INDIA

Kunming ●

Zhu Jiang (Pearl River)

Xi Jiang (West River)

3

PACIFIC OCEAN

BANGLADESH

TAIWAN

INDIA

MYANMAR

VIETNAM

● Hong Kong

Macau

CAMBODIA

Hainan

South China Sea

LAOS

3

△ **The Himalayas** are on the border between Nepal and Xizang Province, or Tibet. They include Mount Everest, the world's tallest mountain (29,029 feet high).

▷ **Hong Kong** was under British control until 1997. It is now a Chinese city. But Hong Kong has kept its own police force, money, and laws. Hong Kong is the wealthiest Chinese city. It is often described as the place where "East meets West."

Mountains and deserts

About two-thirds of China is made up of hills, mountains, and vast deserts in the western half of the country. It is home to some huge mountain ranges. The Himalayas rise along the southwestern border. The high country of Tibet forms a tablelike plain that is up to 13,000 feet high. It is known as "the roof of the world." North of Tibet stretch the majestic peaks of the Kunlun Shan range, one of the longest ranges in Asia.

The Taklan Makan desert is in the northwest, and the Gobi desert stretches up into Mongolia. Most people in China live in the fertile plains in the east of the country and along the coast.

Three Gorges

The Chang Jiang, or Yangtze River, flows 3,859 miles across China, from Tibet in the west to the East China Sea in the east. The Three Gorges Dam was built to store water for the surrounding countryside. It also generates power and helps large ships pass along this great waterway. But building the dam also forced more than one million people to move because the new reservoir flooded their homes. And a very beautiful landscape has disappeared forever.

Flooding

The summer rainy season can cause massive floods. The floods often make millions of people homeless and cause many deaths. The Huang He (Yellow River), Xi Jiang (West River), and Zhu Jiang (Pearl River) also flow

▽ **Inner Mongolia** is a Chinese region that borders (Outer) Mongolia. It has vast deserts, such as the Tenggar and the Hobq. Sandstorms from here can be felt as far away as Colorado in the United States.

from China's mountainous regions. The Yellow River is named for the yellow mud it carries in its waters. As the river snakes across the North China Plain, it leaves this mud, known as "loess," behind. The riverbed rises higher and higher as it silts up. The river embankments, or levees, help protect the land around the river from floods. But the more the riverbed rises, the less protection these flood defenses offer.

▽ **The Three Gorges Dam** is a giant dam on the Yangtze River. It holds enormous amounts of water. Here ships are waiting to pass from one level to another in the Five Steps Ship Lock.

The food we grow in
CHINA

China's many millions of people need plenty of food. The country has large fertile areas where fruit and vegetables can be grown and animals raised. It also has a long shoreline and many rivers with fish and seafood. But there are also vast cold or dry deserts and mountains where little grows.

Northern China

Rice or other cereals are eaten at almost every meal in China. Rice is the main cereal crop. Most rice is grown on small farms, and often directly outside each village. Rice has several harvests a year. The center and the south of China produce the most rice. Where the land is hilly, farmers build level platforms, called terraces, to grow food. They capture rainwater running off the hillsides and guide it into the terraces. The water forms glistening pools in these paddies (rice fields). Growers plant rice seedlings in the paddies. Later the rice is harvested by hand, too. Fried rice is a typical meal from northern China.

▷ **Rice-growing** is back-breaking work. This man holds a bundle of rice stalks. He separates them out and plants the stalks directly in water. People flood fields or terraces on purpose to make such artificial ponds, known as paddies.

△ **These fishermen** use traditional conical nets from their rafts to capture fish and seafood. China is the world's top fishing nation. Its coastlines, rivers, and river mouths are home to more than 200 types of fish and seafood.

Fishing

The Bohai Sea, the Yellow Sea, and the East and South China Sea are dotted with more than 5,000 islands. Many rivers spill out into these waters. They carry important food for sea life. Fishermen there catch crab, shrimps, and octopus. They catch hairtail, croaker, mackerel, herring, flounder, sardines, shark, and anchovy. They also harvest various different seaweeds and algae for food. Many types of freshwater fish are caught in China's lakes and rivers, including carp, bream, eel, catfish, rainbow trout, salmon, whitebait, and mullet. Some fish are also farmed in ponds.

▽ *In Tibet, long-haired cattle,* known as yaks, move around with their nomadic owners.

Grasslands and mountains

Huge numbers of cattle, sheep, and goats graze on the dry, dusty northern grasslands. Many people here are Muslim so they do not eat pork. On bitterly cold days people gather round the traditional Mongolian firepot for a warming lamb or mutton stew. Crops of wheat, barley, millet, and soybeans are grown in the north. Wheat flour is used to make the buns and noodles that people eat every day.

The far west of China is mountainous, so fewer plants can be grown here. In remote places, such as Mongolia, many people are nomadic. Nomads move from place to place to find water and grazing for their animals. At one time, most of China's cattle grazed freely on these pastures.

△ **Fish and shellfish** are caught in the South China Sea. They add to the rich variety of foods at markets in the south of the country.

Warm, fertile center

The provinces of Sichuan and Hunan are famous for their cooking. The weather is warm. Before freezers were invented people had to preserve food by pickling, salting, or drying it. Spices, such as chili, ginger, star anise, and the tangy red Sichuan peppercorns, are important ingredients in many Sichuan dishes, for example in bang-bang chicken.

The fertile farmlands in the east of central China produce large crops of wheat, corn, millet, and sweet potatoes. Rice farmers have two to three harvests of rice a year. Rapeseed, peanuts, and sesame seeds make excellent cooking oils. Snow peas, cabbage, and taro are popular vegetables. Local people enjoy drinking tea, and the hillsides are covered with green, or oolong, teas. Pigs are raised for pork and many small farms keep poultry.

Warm, humid south

The climate in the province of Guangdong is almost tropical, so it is always warm and wet. Many people live in this part of China. The busy capital is Guangzhou, which was once known as Canton. It lies on the banks of the Pearl River delta. Cantonese cookery is famous. Citrus fruit, lychees, mangoes, bananas, and other tropical fruit grow well here. The Cantonese love pork and poultry. They also eat frogs' legs and chicken's feet as treats. In the southern province of Yunnan, pickers gather shoots in tea plantations. They press them into bricks of *toucha* tea.

let's make...
EGG-FRIED RICE

In Northern China we eat fried rice almost every day. My mother adds any number of different ingredients, from egg to pork or shrimps. People in Taiwan also like this dish.

WHAT YOU NEED:

SERVES 4 PEOPLE:

2¼ cups white rice
4 eggs, beaten
light soy sauce
4 tablespoons groundnut
    or soy oil
2 green onions
⅓ cup peeled shrimps
⅓ cup ham
⅓ cup green peas

MY TIP

Use some leftover boiled rice for this recipe. It won't work so well if you use freshly cooked rice, because that's too sticky and gooey. If you don't have any leftover rice, cook some and allow it to cool for a while.

◁ This is a tasty main meal. We often just have a large plate with rice in the middle of the table and we all help ourselves.

1 Put the rice in a saucepan, pour over 3⅓ cups water and leave it to swell up a little. Pour off some of the water so it still stands about ½ inch above the level of the rice. Bring it to a boil, then turn heat to low.

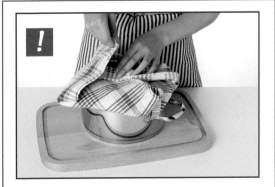

2 Wrap the saucepan lid in a clean cloth and place it on the saucepan. Cook the rice for 10 minutes, without taking the lid off or stirring the rice. Take the pan off the cooker and leave it to cool for at least 1 hour, without lid.

3 Crack the eggs into a bowl. Stir in 2 tablespoons soy sauce. Trim the green onions. Chop the onions, prawns, and ham. Heat 2 teaspoons oil in a wok. Add half the egg and cook until it is set, like an omelet. Take it out. Repeat with the other egg.

4 Cut the two omelets into thin strips. Heat the rest of the oil in the wok. Add the green onions, shrimps, and ham. Fry for 1–2 minutes, stirring with a wooden spoon. Add the cooked rice and fry for 2 minutes. Add the peas and fry for 2 minutes more, stirring. Stir in the omelet strips. Serve with soy sauce in a small bowl.

let's make...
CRISPY SEAWEED

In China, people say that seaweed is a special food, good enough to serve to a king. We never had a king come to our house, but we like serving seaweed to family and friends.

▽ Can you eat crispy seaweed with your chopsticks? It's not easy, and we often just use our fingers!

WHAT YOU NEED:

SERVES 4 PEOPLE:

1 lb of bok choi leaves
(or spring greens)
neutral-tasting oil for
frying, for example
canola oil
½–1 teaspoon salt
2 teaspoons sugar
3 tablespoons
peanuts, pine
kernels, or
flaked
almonds

WHAT'S THIS: seaweed?

Seaweed is a type of algae. There are thousands of different kinds, but only some are good for eating. It comes in different colors (red, brown, or green). You can use any kind of cabbage instead: bok choi or Chinese cabbage are good if you can't find seaweed.

1 Separate all the cabbage leaves. Wash the leaves and cut out the hard stems; throw these away. Pat the leaves dry with paper towels. Place a few leaves on top of each other, then cut them into thin strips with a sharp knife. Spread the strips out. Allow them to dry for 1 hour.

2 Heat plenty of oil in a wok or large skillet. Check if the oil is hot with this trick: hold a wooden spoon into the oil. If small bubbles appear immediately on the spoon, the oil is hot enough.

4 Lift the fried leaves out with a slotted spoon. Put them to drain on plenty of paper towels so the oil can run off. Put the leaves that are finished into a bowl and keep them warm in a low oven (about 180°F). Fry the rest of the leaves.

3 Put a handful of the cabbage leaf strips into the hot oil, and fry them for about 45 seconds. Watch the time—45 seconds is not very long. The leaves should get dark green but they should not burn.

5 When all the leaves are cooked, sprinkle them with the sugar and salt. Chop the groundnuts, pine kernels, or almonds, and sprinkle them on top. Serve and enjoy!

let's make...
BANG-BANG CHICKEN

Why is this dish called bang-bang? Three guesses. Well, in order to flatten the chicken breasts, the chef beats them with a mallet, and that just sounds like ... bang-bang!

WHAT YOU NEED:

SERVES 4 PEOPLE:

4¼ cups chicken stock
4 chicken breasts, without bones and skinned
3 ounces glass noodles, broken into short pieces

1 cucumber
1 carrot
2 green onions
roasted sesame seeds
Sichuan pepper

FOR THE SAUCE

3 ounces smooth, unsweetened peanut butter
3 garlic cloves
1 chili
3 tablespoons light soy sauce
1 handful fresh cilantro

1 tablespoon brown sugar
1 tablespoon rice vinegar
2 tablespoons sesame oil

◁ You can make other dishes with the same sauce, try for example bang-bang shrimps.

WHAT'S THIS: Sichuan pepper?

This is not really a pepper, but the berry of a tree. It looks like other peppercorns but it is red or pink. It tastes hot and lemony, and it makes your mouth tingle.

18

1 Bring the stock to a boil in a saucepan. Add the chicken breasts, turn the heat to low, and cook for about 15 minutes over gentle heat. Lift the chicken breasts out with a slotted spoon and allow them to cool. Cut chicken into thin strips.

2 Put the glass noodles into a bowl. Boil some water and pour it over the noodles. Allow the noodles to soak in the water for 5 minutes.

3 Peel the cucumber and halve it lengthways. Scrape out the seeds with a teaspoon. Cut the halves into thin slices. Peel the carrot. Trim the green onions. Cut both into thin strips.

4 Put all the sauce ingredients into a bowl. Purée everything with a hand-held blender or in a blender. Taste the sauce. Add more salt or pepper if needed.

5 Arrange the vegetables on a large platter. Place the chicken slices on top. Sprinkle with sesame seeds. Grind some Sichuan pepper over the top, and garnish with cilantro. Serve with the sauce.

How we celebrate in
CHINA

Festivals in China often follow the lunar calendar. This yearly calendar is based on the moon. Each month starts with a new moon (when the moon cannot be seen in the sky). The Chinese zodiac names each whole year after an animal. Many Chinese people think that a person has the same qualities as that year's animal. People born in the Year of the Dragon, for example, are said to be short-tempered, energetic, and excitable; monkey people are clever, skilful, and inventive.

Chinese New Year

The New Year is the most important Chinese holiday. It is celebrated by Chinese people around the world. New Year falls on different dates, between late January and mid-February. It starts with the new moon and ends 15 days later. Each day has its own special customs. One of these is the Lion Dance. The lion is a holy animal. Its dance is meant to bring good luck for the new year and to chase away evil.

▷ *The Lion Dance* is part of the New Year's celebrations. The lion's head is made of papier mâché. There are different styles of dancing. In northern China, dancers copy the way a lion moves. But in the south, people move their legs much more and the dancers are martial artists.

Chinese families clean their houses from top to bottom in the days before the New Year. They sweep away all that was bad in the past, and make a fresh start.

Fireworks

People wear red clothes for all celebrations. They give each other red envelopes with money (*lai see*), and they light fireworks that explode in flashes of red. The color red means fire, and people believe that fire burns bad luck. A long time ago, people lit bamboo sticks. Later, in about 800, the Chinese people invented gunpowder. They could now make fireworks, and Chinese fireworks have become famous all over the world. When the lion or dragon dances in a parade, firecrackers are often thrown at his feet to keep him awake.

Lantern Festival

The last day of the New Year's celebrations is known as the Lantern Festival. Many children make their own paper lanterns, and craftworkers produce superb and very complicated lanterns. Most lanterns are red, or have a red in the pattern. Lanterns are often shaped like the animals of the zodiac. They may also look like flowers or people from legends. Some are even made from ice!

Amazing lights can be seen in all the large towns—they even rival the Christmas lights in the United States. During the Lantern Festival there is usually also a lion or dragon dance. The dragon may be up to 100 feet long. Many people dance under the paper costume to keep the dragon moving.

Moon Festival

The Moon or Mid-Autumn Festival is the day in fall when farmers celebrate their harvest. Families get together and admire the bright full moon of that night, which is known as the "harvest moon." They have a nighttime picnic and share specially baked mooncakes. In Hong Kong, people go to the hills so they can see the moon. The festival takes place on the fifteenth day of the eighth moon. This is sometime in late September or early October according to Western calendars.

▽ **Street parades** with costumes, marching bands, and floats are now part of Chinese New Year celebrations in the United States.

Dragon Boat Festival

This exciting boat race takes place in Hong Kong Harbor on the fifth day of the fifth moon (in June). The boats are up to 120 feet long. They have dragons' heads and carry flags. According to legend, they search for Qu Yuan (ca. 340–278 BC), a famous Chinese poet who drowned himself in a river. At the time, people threw dumplings into the water to stop the fish from eating Qu's body. Today people have fun, picnic on the grass banks, and watch the race.

△ *National Day* is celebrated on October 1. It is a political holiday to celebrate the founding of the People's Republic of China in 1949. Public squares and parks in China, Hong Kong, and Macau are beautifully decorated.

let's make...
PORK DUMPLINGS

We eat many kinds of dumpling in China. The dumplings in this recipe are folded over like pockets. One of them contains a surprise. We eat them just after midnight, on the first day of the New Year.

▽ I love dumplings, particularly the ones that contain surprises!

WHAT YOU NEED:

MAKES 25 DUMPLINGS:

1 pack deep-frozen round won ton dough disks (about 3 inches wide)
2 ounces canned bamboo shoots
1 handful fresh cilantro
2 tender green onions
½ lb ground pork
1 garlic clove
1 teaspoon freshly grated ginger
1 tablespoon dark soy sauce
1 tablespoon sesame oil

PLUS:

little surprises (clean coins or small candies)
canola oil for frying

TIME FOR _dumplings_

We eat the dumplings in the new year, but we cook them in the old year. This is so that no knives cut up and destroy the good luck for the new year.

1 Let the wonton circles defrost. Drain bamboo shoots in a sieve. Cut bamboo shoots, cilantro, and green onions into very small pieces. **!**

2 Put the ground pork in a large bowl. Crush the garlic into the bowl, add the grated ginger, soy sauce, and sesame oil. Knead everything together with your (clean) hands.

3 Fill a small bowl with cold water. Take a wonton and moisten its edges with cold water. Put 1 teaspoon of filling into the center. Repeat with the other wontons. Place the surprise on one of the circles.

4 Fold the dough circle over to make a pocket. Press the edges together with your fingers so you get a wavy rim. Slightly flatten the dumpling.

5 In a large skillet, heat plenty of oil and fry the wontons in batches. Place some into the pan next to each other and fry them for 3 minutes. Then carefully turn them over with a wooden spoon. Fry the other side for 3 minutes. Serve.

let's make...
MOONCAKES

Chinese people eat these festival cakes during the Moon Festival in fall. People have great feasts and look at the moon, which is particularly bright during that night.

WHAT YOU NEED:

MAKES 12 CAKES:

3¼ cups self-raising flour
3 teaspoons baking powder
⅔ cup sugar
¾ cup neutral oil
3 eggs, cracked into a bowl
   and lightly beaten
about ⅔ cup cold water

PLUS:

oil or butter for greasing
   the baking dish
about 1 lb sweet red
   bean paste
1 egg, cracked into a bowl
   and beaten for brushing

◁ Mooncakes and the moon itself are symbols of harmony. Some cakes carry a moon print on top, others have a moonlike egg yolk in the center.

WHAT'S THIS: red bean paste?

To make this paste, red azuki beans are boiled, then puréed and sweetened. We use it as a filling in rice balls, pancakes, and in sweet dessert soups.

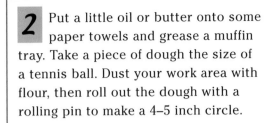

2 Put a little oil or butter onto some paper towels and grease a muffin tray. Take a piece of dough the size of a tennis ball. Dust your work area with flour, then roll out the dough with a rolling pin to make a 4–5 inch circle.

1 Hold a large sieve over a bowl, tip in the flour, and shake gently so it falls into the bowl. Add the sugar, oil, and eggs. Knead everything with your hands or with the kneading hooks of a mixer. The dough should hold together but not be sticky. Add a little more water, until it holds together well.

3 Place each circle in a hollow in the muffin tray so it overhangs. Put 1 tablespoon bean paste in each one. Brush the pastry edges with water.

4 Heat the oven to 400°F. Make 12 walnut-sized balls and roll them out to make 2–3 inch circles. Put the smaller circles on top of the paste in the larger ones. Gently press all around the "lid" to close in the paste.

5 Brush the top of the cakes with the beaten egg. Bake the mooncakes for about 25 minutes.

How we celebrate at home in
CHINA

For the big, national festivals there are fixed dates that are taken from the lunar calendar. But for private celebrations, people usually choose dates. They pick a day that is "auspicious"—this means that it is thought to be a lucky date.

Weddings

In the past, marriages were arranged. They were agreed between the family of the bride and the bridegroom's family. Today most marriages are love matches—the two people want to get married and live together. But people still follow many old customs. The groom has to ask for the woman's hand, and he also gives money to his future in-laws.

Bridal cakes are sent out as invitations. Everyone who has been invited sends back expensive gifts to the bride's family. On the morning of the wedding, the bride serves tea to her parents to show her respect. Later she performs the tea ceremony together with her husband for his parents.

◁ **The bride's hair** is dressed by a "good-luck woman" on the night before the wedding or on the morning of the wedding day. The bride's dress is red. This color brings good luck and joy. She also wears a crown.

Banquets

For many celebrations people get together and have a big meal. Such meals need to be carefully planned because each food has a special meaning. There are always red dishes because red is a lucky color. Fish is usually served because the Chinese word for fish sounds like "plentiful." Long noodles are said to promise a long life, and desserts bring a sweet life. Fish and chicken are served whole to symbolize completeness.

△ **The wedding banquet** is an important meal. The bridegroom's parents pay for the party. They will invite as many people as possible, and make the party as big as they can afford. In the past, wedding banquets were held for up to seven days. Every night, guests and neighbors come back and enjoy more tasty foods together. The meal always has eight courses because eight is a lucky number.

Family birthdays

In China, birthdays are not celebrated in the same way as in Western countries. The only really important birthdays are the very first one—the birth of a child—and every tenth birthday from the age of sixty. In China, a baby is believed to be one year old as soon as it is born. Then it gets one year older each time a new year begins in the lunar calendar.

One month after a baby is born, a first great celebration is held in its honor. Most other birthdays pass almost unnoticed, until

△ *Lai see* are small red envelopes that contain money. Children and adults receive *lai see* as gifts. The first great feast day in the life of a newborn child is the one-month celebration. Family members come to see the baby and give *lai see* envelopes, foods, or gifts of gold or silver items.

an adult has reached the age of sixty and starts his or her "second life."

All the family members, especially the children, give an older person symbolic gifts for their birthdays. The gifts are meant to promise a long and happy life and good health. A typical birthday meal includes longevity (or long-life) noodles—they are meant to grant the birthday person a long life. Again, money in a red-and-gold envelope might be given to the adult.

Name-giving

Finding the right name for a child is complex in China. There are many things to consider. The name is believed to influence the future of the child, and so it needs to have positive meanings. Choosing a name that promises great wealth or a long life is preferred. In China, the last name is mentioned first so John Smith would be called Smith John.

Chinese tea ceremony

Serving tea is an important ritual in China. Generally, pouring the tea for another person shows respect. It means that one regards the other person as more important than oneself. So children serve tea to their parents, for example, and younger people pour tea for an older person. But today the rules have become more relaxed.

▽ **In the Chinese tea ceremony**, small clay cups and pots are used. Different types of tea are served in different pots. The server first warms the pot and the cups with hot water before brewing and pouring the tea.

let's make...
FRIED NOODLES

We call these "longevity noodles," or "long-life noodles." The longer they are, the better, because that means you will have a long life. We eat the noodles for important holidays, or when someone celebrates a special birthday.

▽ I like slurping the noodles, but my Mom is not so happy with that! She says it makes a rude noise—and I often get some sauce on my T-shirt!

WHAT YOU NEED:

SERVES 4 PEOPLE:

2 tablespoons dried shiitake mushrooms
4 ounces long thin rice or egg flour noodles
1 bunch green onions
1 cup snow peas
1 cup peeled shrimps
4 tablespoons oil
4 garlic cloves
2 tablespoons rice vinegar
2 tablespoons oyster sauce
1 tablespoon sweet soy sauce
3 tablespoons light soy sauce
fresh cilantro leaves

WHAT'S THIS: shiitake mushroom?

This is an edible mushroom. It is known in the West by its Japanese name. The mushrooms are very healthy and they are another symbol of longevity.

1 Wash the shiitake mushrooms. Then put them in a small bowl with lukewarm water and allow them to soak for 20 minutes.

2 Put the noodles into a large bowl. Boil up some water and pour it over the noodles. Allow them to swell up. Wash and trim the green onions, then cut them into thin, diagonal pieces.

3 Wash the snow peas. Trim the ends. Cut the peas into slanted strips. Wash and pat dry the shrimps.

4 Take the mushrooms from the bowl and squeeze them out. Twist out the stalks and throw them away. Cut the tops into thin strips.

5 Heat the oil in a wok or skillet. Crush the garlic into the wok and fry for a few seconds. Stir in the green onions and the snow peas, and fry for 1 minute. Add mushrooms and shrimps. Fry for 5 minutes, stirring all the time.

6 Put the oyster sauce and the two soy sauces in a small bowl, and stir together. Pour the sauce into the wok. Drain the noodles in a sieve. Stir them into the wok mixture. Fry for 2–3 minutes. Check the seasoning and sprinkle with cilantro leaves.

WHAT'S THIS: symbolic food?

For us, many foods and symbolic meals have a meaning. Long noodles mean a long life. Dumplings mean wealth. Lettuce stands for riches. And a whole fish is a symbol of togetherness.

let's make...
FORTUNE COOKIES

Each cookie holds a little slip of paper that tells your fortune. Of course, when you make your own, you could write all sorts of things on these slips of paper—good luck messages, birthday greetings, jokes…

▽ I like to write funny messages—ones to make people laugh out loud!

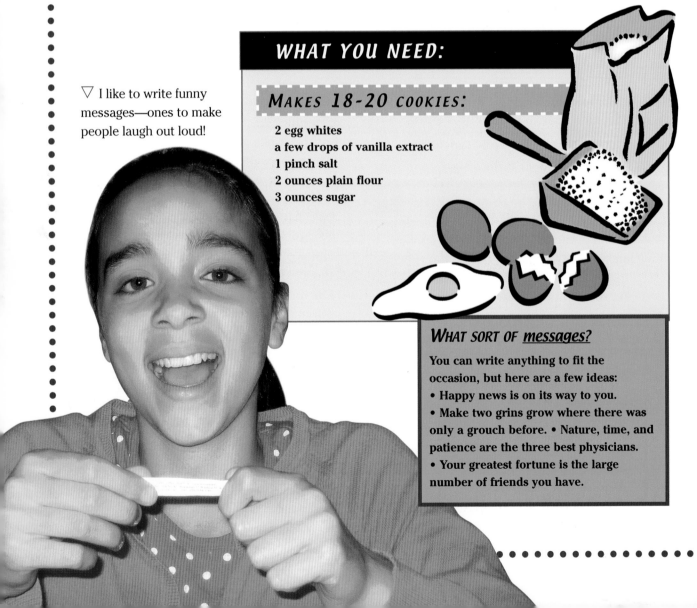

WHAT YOU NEED:

MAKES 18-20 COOKIES:

2 egg whites
a few drops of vanilla extract
1 pinch salt
2 ounces plain flour
3 ounces sugar

WHAT SORT OF *messages*?

You can write anything to fit the occasion, but here are a few ideas:
• Happy news is on its way to you.
• Make two grins grow where there was only a grouch before. • Nature, time, and patience are the three best physicians.
• Your greatest fortune is the large number of friends you have.

1 Write your messages on small slips of paper, about ½ inch by 4 inches. Draw 3-inch circles on two sheets of baking paper, leave plenty of space between circles. Place the sheets upside down on baking trays.

2 Heat the oven to 400°F. In a deep bowl, whisk the egg whites with the vanilla essence using an electric whisk until they are foamy but not stiff. Add salt and sugar, a little at a time, and stir with a spoon. Stir in 1 teaspoon water.

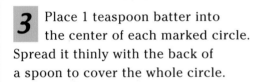

3 Place 1 teaspoon batter into the center of each marked circle. Spread it thinly with the back of a spoon to cover the whole circle.

4 Bake the cookies in the oven for 6 minutes, or until they are light brown at the edge but still pale in the center. Take them out of the oven. Scrape them off the tray with a spatula. Turn them over onto a lightly oiled board.

5 Immediately place a lucky paper onto each cookie. Fold the circles in half so they make half moons. Turn the ends toward the center. Place the cookies in a muffin tray. Allow them to cool completely.

How we live in
CHINA

Families in China tend to be small. That is because parents living in cities are fined if they have more than one child. This rule was introduced in 1979—it was meant to stop the country's huge population from growing too quickly. Family life is traditionally very important in China, so the parents and grandparents lavish lots of attention and gifts on only children.

▽ *People move* to cities such as Suzhou (below) in eastern China in search of jobs and a better standard of living. The cities grow fast, but this also creates problems—people need more electricity and water, and produce more trash.

City life

China's big cities are growing fast. Many people move from the countryside to the towns in search of work. High-rise office buildings, expressways, shops, factories, and apartment blocks spring up like mushrooms and change the city skylines. Entirely new cities are built inland. In a typical city family, both parents go out to work, six days a week. People travel by bus, subway, train, and car, and many people ride bicycles to work.

△ *Schoolchildren* normally wear uniforms, such as a red or blue tracksuit, or blue dresses like the girls above. But in some cities, for example in Shanghai, students are allowed to wear their own clothes for some days.

Country life

China's many different ethnic groups live in different regions, and so life in the countryside varies from place to place. Many people work as peasants on the land and are very poor. People often have no car nor even a bicycle. Their homes are simple, and there are no washing machines, fridges, or bathrooms inside the houses. Families in the country are often larger. Many children have to take time off school to work in the fields.

Life at school

In China, children need to get up bright and early to walk or cycle to school by 7 or 8 A.M. The elementary school day lasts until about 4 P.M. Children go to school six days a week. The school year is divided into two nineteen-week semesters. The main school vacations are in July and August.

At elementary school, Chinese children are taught reading and writing, math, science, music, handicrafts, and ethics.

Pupils also do regular exercises in class to keep fit. They have short breaks between lessons, and a longer lunch break of about two hours. In recent years, more Chinese children have become overweight; so sports have become more important.

食品名称 | 单位 | 单位
香糯玉米 | 个 | 4
羊、牛肉串 | 串 | 5
蘑菇 | 串 | 8
| | 5
| | 5
| 串 | 5
| 串 | 15
| 串 | 15

风味 麻辣烫

酸辣粉 麻辣汤

炸鸡排

△ **Street vendors** line the streets in the cities. They sell a variety of tasty snacks, including dumplings, noodle dishes, and Peking duck. In the mornings stallholders offer deep-fried devils, fried rice, or congee. The snacks normally sell quickly so they are always fresh and tasty.

Time off

Like children everywhere, Chinese children enjoy watching TV. Ping pong, basketball, volleyball, and badminton are all popular in China. Families have only one day off during the working week, so they enjoy going for a stroll in a local park. Here they may watch concerts, dancing, and acrobatic displays.

People love going to the movies and reading gossip about the stars. Rollerskating has also become a big hit in the cities. Most families do not keep any pets because it is expensive to buy a licence. Some children keep tropical fish in an aquarium. In the cities, people also like to visit the zoo and watch the animals.

Meal times

Children start the day with a breakfast of steamed bread, dumplings, or noodles. Deep-fried devils are popular, and congee is a type of porridge. Children have lunch in the school canteen. In the evenings, they eat supper with their families. A typical family meal consists of vegetables, meat, and fish. Fried pork is a favorite food, often with added vegetables. A soup, such as a sweet and sour soup, may be served too. Large platters with different dishes stand in the center of the table, and people help themselves with chopsticks, or spoons for soup. The meal is washed down with tea, China's national drink.

▽ **Restaurants** in China are visited only by richer families or business people. Most places serve only Chinese food, but there are some Korean and Japanese restaurants.

HUNG KEE SEAFOOD RESTAURANT

HUNG KEE RESTAURANT

WRITING CHINESE

Mandarin Chinese is written in little groups of lines that are known as characters. Each character represents part of a word and has a meaning of its own. By the time Chinese children leave school they have learned to write about 8,000 characters. New characters can be invented any time. They are often made up of two others.

let's make...
DEEP-FRIED DEVILS

For Sunday breakfast, Mom usually makes *yu za kuei*, which means "deep-fried devils." They're a bit like Mexican churros. We dip the devils into congee, which is a type of porridge, or into flavored soy milk.

▽ These devils taste devilishly good! And you can eat them as you go.

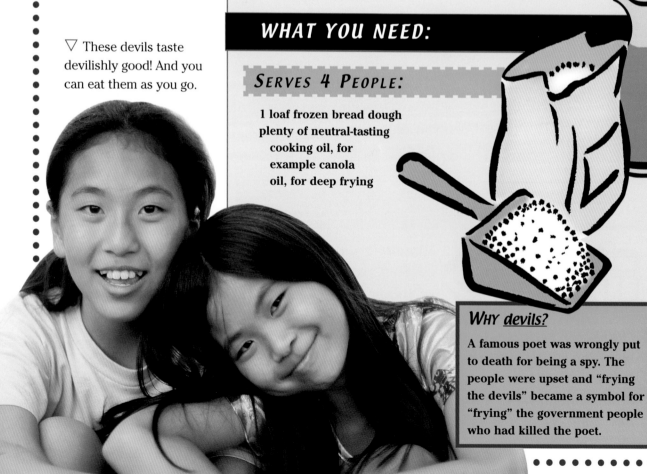

WHAT YOU NEED:

SERVES 4 PEOPLE:

1 loaf frozen bread dough
plenty of neutral-tasting
    cooking oil, for
    example canola
    oil, for deep frying

WHY <u>devils</u>?

A famous poet was wrongly put to death for being a spy. The people were upset and "frying the devils" became a symbol for "frying" the government people who had killed the poet.

1 Cover the dough with a cloth and allow it to defrost overnight in the fridge. Take the dough out of the fridge about 1 hour before you are ready to make the devils.

3 Heat the oil for deep-frying in a wok. Hold the handle of a wooden spoon into the oil. If small bubbles rise on the handle, the oil is hot enough. **!**

2 Divide the dough into 24 equal parts. Roll each piece between your hands to form a long sausage shape. Allow the shapes to rest for 1 hour, at room temperature.

CAN I MAKE THE dough MYSELF?

Stir together 1 ounce fresh yeast, ½ cup lukewarm water, and a pinch of sugar. Cover and allow to rest for a few minutes. Add another ½ cup water, 1 lb flour, 4 tablespoons olive oil, and 1 teaspoon salt. Knead to make a smooth dough. Cover and allow to rest for 1 hour at room temperature. Now the dough is ready for making devils!

4 Take each sausage with both hands. Pull it a little and twist the ends in opposite directions as you pull. Place the twisted piece in the oil and fry until it is golden brown. Lift it out with a slotted spoon and drain on paper towels. Repeat until all the devils are fried.

let's make...
HOT & SOUR SOUP

This soup is from Sichuan in southern China. People there eat spicy dishes. They add heat to a dish with fresh chilies or chili oil, grind in Sichuan peppers, or use a ready-made chili sauce.

▽ I can't get enough of this soup! Chili and ginger are also said to help against colds. Well, that's my excuse for a second helping!

WHAT YOU NEED:

SERVES 4 PEOPLE:

4 dried shiitake mushrooms
6 ounces tofu
1 small can bamboo shoots
  (4 ounces)
5 ounces chicken breast
  (skinned and boned)
5 cups chicken broth
2 tablespoons light soy sauce
2–3 tablespoons spicy garlic
  chili sauce
2–3 tablespoons rice vinegar
2 tablespoons cornstarch
1 egg, beaten
2 teaspoons sesame oil
1 green onion

WHAT'S THIS: tofu?

Tofu is a beancurd. It is made from squashed soybeans and looks like yogurt. Tofu can be fried, baked, or eaten raw. It is used in many Asian dishes, and is very popular with vegetarians.

1 Put the mushrooms into a bowl and add plenty of warm water. Allow them to soak for 20 minutes.

2 Twist out the mushroom stalks and throw them away. Cut the tops into thin strips. Cut the tofu, bamboo shoots, and chicken into small cubes. **!**

3 Put the broth into a large saucepan. Add the soy sauce and the garlic chili sauce to spice it. Add the mushrooms, bamboo shoots, and the chicken. Turn the heat to low and simmer for 5 minutes.

4 Put the cornstarch into a cup, add a little cold water, and stir with a spoon to combine. Stir the mixture into the soup. Add the tofu and vinegar. Bring back to a boil. Now slowly drizzle in the egg. It sets in the soup in little lumps. Drizzle the sesame oil on top. Trim and chop the green onion and sprinkle it over the soup. Serve. **!**

WHICH mushrooms?

If you can find them, try using tiger lily buds or cloud-ear mushrooms in this soup instead of shiitake mushrooms. Prepare them in the same way.

let's make...
FRIED PORK WITH SCALLIONS

A quick stir-fry is what we eat most evenings. You can include just about anything, from meat and fish or shrimps, to all kinds of vegetables. This is a family favorite.

WHAT YOU NEED:

SERVES 4 PEOPLE:

6 tablespoons sweet soy sauce
8 tablespoons fish sauce
3 red chilies, trimmed and chopped
4 garlic cloves, peeled and chopped
⅔ cup vegetable stock
1½ teaspoons cornstarch
1 lb pork (escalope or fillet)
2 red bell peppers
1–2 bunches scallions

4 tablespoons cooking oil, for example canola
fresh parsley to garnish

◁ I particularly like the crunchy vegetables. They have lots more flavor than boiled vegetables.

WHAT'S THIS: fish sauce?

Fish sauce is made from fermented fish. It makes food taste salty, not fishy. If you can't find any fish sauce in the stores, just add a little salt instead.

1 In a bowl, stir together the soy sauce with the fish sauce, chilies, garlic, stock, and cornstarch.

3 Wash the bell peppers. Halve them, cut out the stalks, the seeds, and the white skins. Cut the flesh of the peppers into diamond shapes. Wash and trim the green onions. Throw away yellow leaves. Cut onions into slim, diagonal rings.

2 Cut the pork into thin slices, then cut each slice into squares, but not too small. Put the pork in the bowl with the soy mixture, and turn the meat so the pieces are covered with the liquid all over. Cover the dish with a cloth and allow to marinate for 20 minutes.

4 Heat the oil in a wok or deep skillet. Add the scallions and the bell peppers. Stir and fry for about 4 minutes. Push all fried ingredients to the edge of the wok.

5 Take the meat out of the soy sauce and pat it dry. Put a few pieces at a time into the center of the wok. Stir and fry for 2 minutes, then push to the outside. When everything is fried, stir it all together. Add the sauce. Stir and fry for 2–3 minutes more. Transfer to a bowl, garnish with fresh parsley, and serve.

Look it up
CHINA

chopsticks pairs of sticks, the main eating tool in China and other Asian countries; they are usually thinner at one end and can be made from bamboo, bone, metal, plastic, or ivory; the sticks are held in one hand, between thumb and middle and forefinger to pick up items of food

fish sauce a common ingredient in Asian dishes, for example in Chinese soups; it is made from fish but tastes mainly salty

lai-see small red envelopes containing money; they are given to children for New Year, or to brides and grooms, or to friends as gifts

lunar month in China, a new month begins at midnight of the new moon; that is when you cannot see the moon in the sky; today the lunar calendar is only used for deciding festival dates, for finding lucky days for weddings, and for the zodiac

shiitake a type of Chinese mushroom; other types include tiger lily buds and cloud-ear mushrooms

Sichuan pepper a berry that is used in many South Chinese dishes; it is not hot like other peppers, but leaves a special tingly feeling in the mouth; it tastes slightly lemony

stir-frying a common method of cooking food in China and other Asian countries; food is fried in a very hot wok while stirring; when it is cooked, the food is pushed to the edge, and more ingredients are added to the wok

tofu a beancurd made from soybeans; it is white and bland-tasting, but takes on the flavors of other foods

wok a deep round skillet, usually made from cast-iron; it is used for stir-frying food over a high heat

Find out more
CHINA

Books to read

Simonds, Nina and Swartz, Leslie.
**Moonbeams, Dumplings & Dragon Boats:
A Treasury of Chinese Holiday Tales,
Activities & Recipes.**
Boston: The Children's Museum, Gulliver
Books, 2002.

Fry, Ying Ying and Klatzkin, Amy.
Kids Like Me in China.
Yeong & Yeong Book Company, 2001.

Zemlicka, Shannon.
Colors of China.
Carolrhoda Books, 2001.

So, Sungwan.
C Is for China.
Frances Lincoln; reprint 2004.

Web sites to check out

www.infoplease.com/ipa/A0107411.html
General information on China

**www3.nationalgeographic.com/places/
countries/country_china.html**
General information, facts, history, and the
environment in China, from National
Geographic

www.index-china-food.com
All about Chinese food

**www.historyforkids.org/learn/china/food/
index.htm**
About the history of foods in China

http://chinesefood.about.com
All about Chinese food, culture,
and recipes

**http://library.thinkquest.org/3614/
funfacts.htm**
Amusing facts about China

Index
CHINA